FRANKLIN PARK PUBLIC LIBRARY
FRANKLIN PARK, IL.

john green

johngreen

STAR AUTHOR, VLOGBROTHER, and NERDFIGHTER

eric braun

Lerner Publications • Minneapolis

For Henry. Thanks for introducing me to John Green.

Lerner Publications Company
A division of Lerner Publishing Group, Inc.
241 First Avenue North
Minneapolis, MN USA 55401

J-B
GREEN
450-1196

For reading levels and more information, look up this title at www.lernerbooks.com.

The images in this book are used with the permission of: © Alexander Tamargo/Getty Images, pp. 2, 38; © David Livingston/Getty Images, p. 6; © Todd Strand/Independent Picture Service, pp. 8, 19, 21, 23, 26, 28, 29, 30; © Joshua Sudock/The Orange County Register/ZUMPAPRESS.com/Alamy, p. 9; © Sarah Bosserman, p. 10; © iStockphoto.com/rgaydos, p. 11; © Fotosearch/Getty Images, p. 12; © Brian Gray/Getty Images, p. 14; © Ed Kashi.National Geographic/Getty Images, p. 15; © marchello74/iStock/Thinkstock, p. 17; © AF Archive/Alamy, p. 18; © Jim Spellman/WireImage/Getty Images, p. 20; © McO'River, p. 24; © Everett Collection Inc/Alamy, p. 25 (top); © Media 24/Gallo Images/Getty, p. 25 (middle); © Dinodia Photos/Getty Images, p. 25 (bottom); © Rick Diamond/Getty Images for Allied, p. 27; Gage Skidmore/Wikimedia Commons (cc 3.0), p. 31; © Lily Lawrence/WireImage/Getty Images, p. 33; © Rick Diamond/Getty Images for Allied, p. 34; AP Photo/Matt Sayles/Invision for Buzzfeed, p. 36; AP Photo/20th century Fox/James Bridges, p. 37.

Front cover: © Horizons WWP/Alamy.

Main body text set in Rotis Serif Std 55 Regular 13.5/17. Typeface provided by Adobe Systems.

Library of Congress Cataloging-in-Publication Data

Braun, Eric.
    John Green : star author, vlogbrother, and nerdfighter / by Eric Braun.
       pages   cm. — (Gateway Biographies)
    Includes bibliographical references and index.
    ISBN 978-1-4677-7244-0 (lib. bdg. : alk. paper)
    ISBN 978-1-4677-7571-7 (pbk.)
    ISBN 978-1-4677-7261-7 (EB pdf)
    1. Green, John, 1977–Juvenile literature. 2. American authors–21st century–Biography–
Juvenile literature. I. Title.
PS3607.R432928Z55 2015
813'.6—dc23 [B]   2014023635

Manufactured in the United States of America
1 – DP – 12/31/14

Contents

A YOUNG NERD 10

QUESTIONS ABOUT
SUFFERING AND FAITH 14

BECOMING AN AUTHOR 16

BROTHERHOOD 2.0 21

THE FAULT IN OUR STARS 28

FROM THE LITTLE SCREEN
TO THE BIG SCREEN 35

IMPORTANT DATES 40

SOURCE NOTES 42

SELECTED BIBLIOGRAPHY 45

FURTHER READING 47

INDEX 48

John Green poised to sign a copy of his runaway hit novel
The Fault in Our Stars

It started with a simple tweet. On the afternoon of June 28, 2011, John Green announced to his 1.1 million Twitter followers the title of his new novel: *The Fault in Our Stars*. He included a link where they could preorder it. An hour later, he tweeted again, promising to sign every copy that was preordered.

The book would not be published for months yet, and in fact, it wasn't even finished. Still, Green's announcement lit up the Internet. While he sat in his office on that early summer day, his fans retweeted the title. They talked about it on Tumblr, Twitter, Facebook, and other platforms. They created covers for the book and posted them online. They preordered it, and they urged their friends to preorder it too.

The Fault in Our Stars began to climb best-seller lists. Green tracked the sales ranking on Amazon. He had published five novels, achieving decent sales and reviews. But he'd never had the kind of runaway success that other

YA (young adult) authors, such as J. K. Rowling, Suzanne Collins, and Stephenie Meyer, had seen. While their books featured magic, dystopian worlds, and vampires, his books were about regular people in the real world. He never imagined his books would get the kind of attention those books did.

Yet every time he refreshed the Amazon page for his book, the sales had increased—a lot. Green realized that something big was happening. Something amazing. Within eight hours, *The Fault in Our Stars* was the No. 1 book on Amazon.

No. 1! John Green still sat in his office. Everything looked the same. But his life had just changed profoundly. With those two tweets, he had become the author of a blockbuster best seller. Giddy with excitement, Green posted a video of himself doing a "happy dance" on his YouTube channel.

John Green ✔
@realjohngreen   ⚙   +👤 Follow

Wow! THE FAULT IN OUR STARS is the #1 bestselling book on Amazon. Unbelievable. Thank you guys. You can preorder here: dft.ba/tfios

Green posted this grateful tweet to fans after learning his book was No. 1 on Amazon.

John Green (*left*) and his brother, Hank, have a large following on YouTube.

He was used to a certain amount of fame. There were those 1.1 million Twitter followers. His YouTube channels, where he'd posted nearly nine hundred videos with his brother, Hank, had more than half a million subscribers. The videos were the reason most of his fans followed him. Those fans—mostly teenagers known as Nerdfighters, a word Green coined and that his smart and free-spirited devotees use to describe themselves—were extremely loyal. Green knew that whatever success he had, he owed to them. "What it tells me is that I'm a lucky guy," Green said when a reporter asked about the explosion of sales.

So how many books would he have to sign? His previous novel had about 1,200 preorders, which was a lot, but he figured he could sign that many in a few days. When his publisher told him that he had to sign 150,000 copies to keep his promise, he was stunned. He knew that it would take more than a few days to pull that off! But he didn't try to back out. He had made a promise.

He got to work in his home in Indianapolis. He signed while watching TV and while making videos. Sometimes his wife sat next to him and added a drawing of a yeti to the page—an inside joke for Green fans. Green often likened his wife to a yeti (a mythical creature that people say is very rarely seen) because he mentioned her in his videos yet she'd never appeared in one.

This signed copy of *The Fault in Our Stars* features a yeti drawn by Green's wife.

Green set about his task with great determination. Over the course of the next several weeks, he signed every copy. The repetitive stress of signing damaged a nerve in his arm, requiring physical therapy. But it was worth it. It was for the Nerdfighters.

A YOUNG NERD

When John Green was born on August 24, 1977, he was brought into a home that was in the process of being emptied. Just three weeks after his birth, his parents moved the family out of their home in Indianapolis. After settling in Orlando, Florida, John's dad, Mike, took a job as the state director of the Nature Conservancy. His mom, Sydney, stayed home with John and his brother, Hank, who was born when John was three. Later, she worked as a community organizer.

John's parents taught him to have empathy and to help others. They also taught him to think for himself and to contemplate philosophical topics, such as the meaning of life and what it meant to be a good person. John, his parents, and his brother often debated these topics at the dinner table.

John loved to read and, among other books, happened to enjoy the Baby-Sitters Club series—titles whose biggest fan base was young girls. He didn't understand why more

John grew up in Orlando, Florida.

boys didn't read these books, which he thought featured great stories. He also read the classic Florida novel *Their Eyes Were Watching God* while he was in school. It became one of his favorite books.

Before long he was writing stories of his own and dreaming of becoming an author, though the dream seemed unrealistic to him. He believed that becoming a published author would be a very big long shot. By the age of ten, he had written his first two books: *It Just Isn't Fair*, about a kid who gets teased, and an anti-bullying book titled *Me and Mitch Learned a Lesson.*

John had two close friends in his neighborhood, Andy and Matt, and he spent a lot of time with them. But while his home life was happy, hanging out with his family and Matt and Andy, he hated going to school. Kids there bullied him relentlessly.

To make matters worse, John struggled in school. His parents and teachers kept telling him he was smart, but his grades were poor. He wasn't good at sports either. The only sports trophy he received was one his parents had made with the inscription "All-Star in Our Hearts."

Grades and sports didn't matter as much to John as being popular. He wanted desperately to have a lot of friends. Instead, the bullying persisted.

Throughout middle school, John was miserable. He was depressed. He sometimes even fantasized about hurting the people who bullied him. Eventually, he transferred to a school called Indian Springs. It was a boarding school in Alabama, and it gave John a chance for a brand-new start.

At Indian Springs, John met students who, like him, loved books. They talked about their favorite authors, such as J. D. Salinger, Michael Chabon, and Toni Morrison. They also wrote poetry and discussed philosophers such as Friedrich Nietzsche. Being around people who cared about the things he did energized John. He still didn't do well in class—he was more concerned with having fun with his friends. But at last, he felt as if he fit in. He wanted to enjoy it as much as possible.

Twice John entered the school's creative writing contest, and twice he came in second. Two of his teachers encouraged him. They believed in his writing and told him to keep working.

Then something happened that affected John deeply: Another student at his school was killed in a car accident. Though he wasn't close to the girl who had died, he knew her, and he later said he felt haunted by "the forever of it."

"I just felt so bad for her," he said. "I *still* feel so bad for her."

QUESTIONS ABOUT SUFFERING AND FAITH

After graduating from high school in 1995, John Green headed to Kenyon College in Ohio with only one book: Allen Ginsberg's *Howl and Other Poems*. He majored in English and religious studies.

The friends and professors Green met at Kenyon liked his energy. He was funny, friendly, and always thinking. He was also always talking, discussing big issues—just like his family did when he was young—and telling stories. He still wanted to be a writer, and he took a class with the novelist P. F. Kluge. Kluge encouraged him but also pushed him. When Green was turned down for an advanced writing course, Kluge consoled his devastated student. But he also said, "Your writing isn't that great." Yet the professor told him, "The stories that you tell during the . . . break—if you could write the way you told *those* stories, then you would write well."

John attended Kenyon College in Ohio, pursuing degrees in English and religious studies.

Novelist P. F. Kluge (*right*) was John's professor at Kenyon College. He encouraged John to become a better writer.

Green was still disappointed he didn't get into the course. But his professor's words helped him understand something. If he wanted to be a writer, he'd have to work harder.

By the time Green graduated from Kenyon, his passion had changed. He'd decided he wanted to be an Episcopal priest. He was accepted to divinity school at the University of Chicago, but before going to Chicago, he worked for several months as a chaplain at a children's hospital in Ohio. His job was to counsel the families of children who had died or were dying.

The experience was extremely painful for Green. "It was difficult and traumatic," he said later. "I've never done anything harder than sitting with a parent as their child died. That happened every day."

One day a two-year-old girl came in with her head badly injured after falling from a high chair. A few minutes later, Green met the girl's father, who was distraught. He helped the dad calm down and then prayed with him. When the prayer was finished, the man shouted, "She fell! It was an accident!"

The little girl later died. Her dad eventually admitted that it wasn't an accident—he had caused the injury that killed her. Green was devastated by the news. He began to ask himself hard questions about his faith. "I found myself really unfulfilled by the answers that are traditionally offered to questions of why some people suffer and why others suffer so little," he said later. He also realized that he hated this man. Just as Green had fantasized about hurting his bullies when he was a teenager, he dreamed of hurting him.

Green decided that he could not be a priest. In addition to the questions he had about religion, he knew that a priest can't be hateful. A priest should want peace for everyone. But Green had too much anger.

BECOMING AN AUTHOR

Green moved to Chicago, but he didn't attend divinity school as he'd planned. Instead, he found a job with *Booklist*, a magazine that reviews books for librarians. He started with a job entering data but was soon promoted to reviewing books.

As he read books and wrote about them for the magazine, his dream of being a writer was reignited. In

Green moved to Chicago in his twenties and took a job at *Booklist*.

particular, he wanted to write a YA novel about the kids he saw in the hospital. But the material he wrote, which was about kids with cancer, wasn't very good. Looking back later, he called that first attempt at a novel "super embarrassing."

Before long, Green became close with Ilene Cooper, an editor at *Booklist*, and Bill Ott, the editor in chief. He told Cooper about an idea he had for a novel about kids in a boarding school much like Indian Springs. She thought it was a good idea and suggested that he write it.

Green's early attempts at the novel were difficult, mostly because he struggled to make up fiction—instead, he mostly told stories about what really happened to him and his friends at Indian Springs. Meanwhile, his depression came back. His longtime girlfriend broke up with him on September 12, 2001. It was the day after terrorists drove planes into the World Trade Center in New York City; the Pentagon in Arlington, Virginia; and a Pennsylvania farm field, killing almost three thousand people. Crushed by both his personal situation and the events of September 11, Green called in sick to work and didn't eat or drink anything but Sprite for several days.

Green called his parents, and they all decided he should come home and get therapy. He went to the *Booklist* office to quit his job, but his boss convinced him to take two weeks off instead and then come back. Maybe he would feel better and want to stay with the magazine.

On his way out, Green found a note from Bill Ott on his desk. It said: "John, I stopped by to say good-bye. I hope all goes well and you're back here in two weeks with an appetite that would put a longshoreman to shame. Now more than ever: Watch *Harvey*."

Harvey is a 1950 black-and-white movie about a man who's friends with a giant, invisible rabbit. Ott had suggested before that Green watch the silly film, which was Ott's favorite movie.

Green drove from Chicago to Orlando with his dad, and over the next two weeks, he went to daily

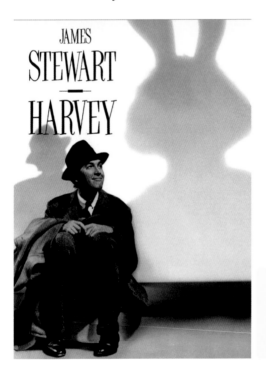

JAMES STEWART — HARVEY

Green credits the movie *Harvey* with helping him through a dark time in his life.

therapy and found better medication. He also watched *Harvey*. "I woke up the morning after watching *Harvey* feeling a little bit better," Green said of watching the movie. "And in all the years since, I have never felt quite as hopeless as I did before I watched *Harvey*."

Things did seem to improve for Green after that. He returned to *Booklist*. And in time, he handed the first draft of a novel called *Looking for Alaska* to Ilene Cooper.

Cooper told him the manuscript was promising. She edited it and sent him back to rewrite, which he did. Green was thrilled, but he kept his expectations low. As a book reviewer he'd seen a lot of great books have poor sales.

The first time he met with his editor at Dutton, she asked him what he hoped for the book. He said he hoped it would sell out in hardcover. She, however, said she'd like it to win the Printz Award—the American Library Association's annual award given to the best book for teens.

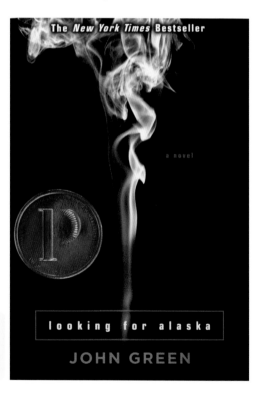

The New York Times Bestseller

a novel

looking for alaska

JOHN GREEN

Looking for Alaska was Green's first published novel.

Looking for Alaska was a semiautobiographical novel about a smart, sensitive kid who goes to a boarding school. Like Green, he is bullied, and like Green, he makes close friends who help him feel accepted. One of those friends is a girl named Alaska.

In the months before *Looking for Alaska* was published, Green became acquainted with a former schoolmate from Indian Springs, Sarah Urist, who also lived in Chicago. They didn't know each other while in high school and happened to connect through a mutual acquaintance. The two grew close and began dating. On an April day in 2005, Green asked Sarah to marry him. She gladly said yes. The same day, she was accepted to graduate school in New York, and—though it meant Green would give up his job at *Booklist*—the two made plans to move there.

Green attends a *Fault in Our Stars* event with his wife, Sarah.

A few months later, Green and Sarah were shopping in New York with Green's parents, who were visiting, when Green got a call on his cell phone. It was someone from the Printz Award committee. Green learned he'd won the Printz Award! On a street corner in New York, he began jumping up and down with joy. His dad took pictures on his cell phone.

BROTHERHOOD 2.0

Green had already begun writing his next novel, another coming-of-age story called *An Abundance of Katherines*, which was published in September 2006. Around this time, he also learned that his work was being taught in classrooms. Green called this the most important thing that had ever happened in his professional life. Teens began contacting him to tell him how much his writing meant to them.

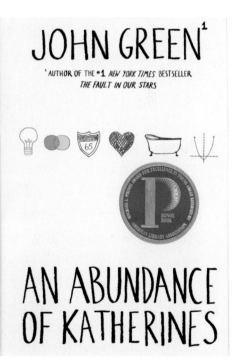

An Abundance of Katherines **had a profound effect on many Green fans.**

He texted and e-mailed with his brother, Hank, who lived in Missoula, Montana, where he ran a website about green energy. The brothers were in regular communication, but they really only saw each other once a year. Because he'd left home for Indian Springs when Hank was ten, Green didn't feel as though he knew his brother very well.

He wanted to change that. He felt that communicating by text was too impersonal, and if they wanted to get to know each other as adults, they needed to see each other. One way to do that was by video. Hank agreed, and the two of them came up with a plan to communicate by video blog, or vlog, every weekday for an entire year. No e-mailing, texting, or other textual communication was allowed.

They called the plan Brotherhood 2.0. Though neither of them had ever edited video before, on January 1, 2007, Hank uploaded his first vlog to YouTube. "Starting on January 1st, today, I will send you a video blog," Hank said in the video. "Tomorrow, you will reply to that video blog. We will continue like this until the year is up."

On January 2, John had to call Hank to ask him how to edit and upload his video. Brotherhood 2.0 was under way.

The vlogs didn't have to be about important topics, such as the ones they had talked about at the dinner table when they were kids. Often, Hank and John simply told each other what they were doing and what they'd been thinking about. John told Hank about getting a haircut from the same barber who cut Bill Clinton's hair. Hank sang songs he'd written.

The Brotherhood 2.0 vlog started on January 1, 2007.

Sometimes big issues did come up, such as politics and the environment. But the videos never got heavy-handed, sentimental, or preachy. They were characterized by the brothers' quick talking and quick wit. Filled with hyper energy and urgency, the videos were fun to watch. The Brotherhood 2.0 YouTube channel slowly started to gain subscribers.

On February 1, John posted a video in which he is stuck in the airport in Savannah, Georgia. In between talking about missing his wife and making jokes about all the golfers in the airport, he finds an arcade and plays a video game called *Aero Fighters*. But he misread the stylized writing on the game and called it *Nerdfighters*.

On February 17, John posted a video from Houston, where he brought up the game again, which he'd seen in another airport. He riffed on what it would be like if the game really was called *Nerdfighters* rather than *Aero Fighters*. He asked Hank, "Is Nerdfighters a game about people who fight against nerds, or is it a game about nerds who fight against other people? I've come to believe that *Nerdfighters* is a game about nerds who fight. Nerds who tackle the scourge of popular people." He went on to describe different nerd characters, such as the band geek and the theater nerd, and their special powers.

He continued on: "To be honest, I've never really understood the war between the nerds and popular

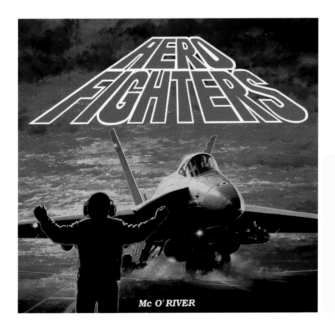

Mc O' RIVER

John misread the name of the arcade game *Aero Fighters* as *Nerdfighters*. Fans soon adopted the term to describe themselves.

people." He compared the two sides. The popular people have George W. Bush and Tom Brady. But, he said, the nerds have Bill Clinton, Abraham Lincoln, Franklin Delano Roosevelt, and "the thinking man's football player, Tiki Barber." The nerds also have Isaac Newton, William Shakespeare, Blaise Pascal, Albert Einstein, Immanuel Kant, Aristotle, Jane Austen, Bill Gates, Mahatma Gandhi, Nelson Mandela, "and all four Beatles. We win!" He ended the video with a song he'd written about the greatness of nerds.

By summer they had 202 subscribers. Then, in July, Hank uploaded a vlog with a song he'd written about Harry Potter. Titled "Accio Deathly Hallows," the song was about how hard it was to wait for the final Harry Potter book, *Harry Potter and*

In Green's imagined war between nerds and popular people, his winning nerd team would include Abraham Lincoln (*top*), Nelson Mandela (*middle*), and Mahatma Gandhi (*bottom*).

Hank Green's song titled "Accio Deathly Hallows" drastically increased the vlogbrothers' viewership.

the Deathly Hallows, to be published. The video got more views than anything they'd posted yet, and overnight Brotherhood 2.0 jumped to seven thousand subscribers.

As the number of followers increased, a community began to form. The followers loved the humor of "vlogbrothers" as well as their strong belief in the value of being smart, sensitive, and compassionate. Followers began to call themselves Nerdfighters. By this time, it was not really about being "against" the popular people anymore. Being a Nerdfighter meant being *for* things that others might consider nerdy. In fact, Nerdfighters were largely positive and supportive. Their rallying cry was, "Don't forget to be awesome," or DFTBA for short.

Nerdfighters hold up a sign featuring an acronym of their motto, "Don't forget to be awesome."

Toward the end of the year, John and Hank realized that with the enthusiasm of the Nerdfighters, they had the power to do something good. They encouraged Nerdfighters to create innovative videos promoting their favorite charities and upload them on December 17. Nerdfighters were then encouraged to "comment spam" the videos—or to comment on them as much as possible. At that time, videos that received lots of comments on YouTube would be promoted to the YouTube "browse page." The intent was to "take over" YouTube for this day with nothing but videos about charities.

They called it the Project for Awesome. Their goal was simply to "decrease world suck," as John and Hank like to say of any action that helps the world. As the videos gained views on the YouTube browser page, the Project for Awesome took in money for the charities they promoted. The Project for Awesome was a big success, raising awareness and money for charities all around the world.

Brotherhood 2.0 was a one-year agreement, but at the end of 2007, the brothers decided to keep going. They changed the name of their video project from Brotherhood 2.0 to vlogbrothers. Every December they do the Project for Awesome.

THE FAULT IN OUR STARS

John Green kept writing—his novel *Paper Towns* came out in 2008. A novel he cowrote with the YA author David Levithan, *Will Grayson, Will Grayson*, came out in 2010. But Green was still thinking about those kids with terminal illnesses he'd met at the hospital years ago. He still wanted to write about them. He tried telling the story from the point of view of a young chaplain, as he had been, but the right story continued to be hard to nail down.

In May 2009, Green attended LeakyCon, a convention in Boston for

#1 *NEW YORK TIMES* BESTSELLING AUTHOR

JOHN GREEN

PAPER TOWNS

Paper Towns is Green's thoughtful take on the mystery novel.

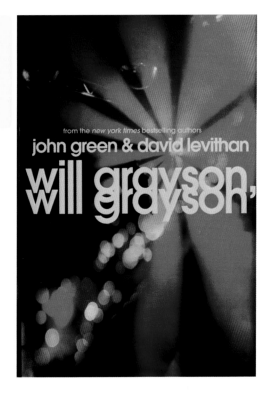

Green and David Levithan cowrote the popular novel *Will Grayson, Will Grayson.*

fans of the Harry Potter books. At a dance during the convention, he met a fifteen-year-old girl with thyroid cancer named Esther Grace Earl. Esther was a Nerdfighter who'd devoured Green's books. She was also a vlogger. Because neither Green nor Esther liked dancing, the two of them talked for a long time in the back of a room while others danced.

Green stayed in touch with Esther after he went home. By this time, he and Sarah lived in Indianapolis, the city where he was born. He appreciated the quiet there after living amid the noise and social pressure of New York. He and Esther became close friends. When Esther died in 2010 at the age of sixteen, Green was once again crushed by the unfairness of the world.

But he was also inspired by the way Esther lived her life. She was sarcastic, angry, brave—and funny. "Esther was such a normal kid and so charismatic," he said. "She

John Green, Esther Grace Earl, and Esther's brother Graham goof off for the camera.

drew me out of myself and my expectations for what illness was and helped me see things in a broader way."

Green began to think in a new way about his old idea for a novel about kids with cancer. The chaplain dropped out of the picture, and a new voice emerged, that of Hazel Grace Lancaster, a girl inspired by Esther's humor and strength (though Green has been clear that Hazel is not Esther). After all this time, he began to unlock the story he'd wanted to tell so badly.

"Walking out of the hospital in 2000 [after deciding not to become a chaplain], I knew I wanted to write a story about sick kids," Green said. "But I was so angry, so furious with the world that these terrible things could happen, and they weren't even rare or uncommon, and I think in the end for the first ten years or so I never could write it because I was just too angry, and I wasn't able to capture the complexity of the world. I wanted the book to be funny. I wanted the book to be unsentimental. After meeting Esther, I felt very differently about whether a short life could be a rich life."

Green worked on his new book while continuing to record vlogbrothers videos. In 2010 he and Sarah had a son, Henry. That year John and Hank created and hosted a convention for people who make and love online videos. Held in Los Angeles, the first VidCon sold out, with about fourteen hundred attendees. It featured presentations and Q&As with video creators as well as bands and dances.

Hank and John Green (*right*) speak at the third annual VidCon, a convention they cofounded for people who enjoy making online videos.

Finally, Green finished *The Fault in Our Stars* and sent it to his editor, Julie Strauss-Gabel. He said writing it was the most "physically and emotionally draining" writing experience of his life.

The book is narrated by Hazel Grace Lancaster, a sixteen-year-old girl with thyroid cancer who, like Green's friend Esther, depends on an oxygen tank. Also like Esther, Hazel is smart, with a wicked sense of humor.

At the beginning of the novel, Hazel meets Augustus Waters at a cancer support group. Augustus had osteosarcoma, but he is now cancer-free after having his leg amputated. The two read each other's favorite novels. Hazel's is called *An Imperial Affliction*, about a girl with terminal cancer. Hazel and Augustus take a trip to Amsterdam to meet the author of *An Imperial Affliction*, which turns out to be a big disappointment. But along the way, Hazel and Augustus fall in love.

After Strauss-Gabel read the manuscript, she and Green talked. They both believed the book would be something special. In fact, Strauss-Gabel felt it could be a big seller with crossover appeal—meaning it might be read by people who don't normally read YA. She and the publishing team felt that girls, boys, and adults would all read it. They gave it a cover that would appeal to all those groups.

Part of the reason *The Fault in Our Stars* felt like a hit in the making was that it defied categorization. It was appealing on many different levels. It was about much more than love and cancer. And for a novel largely about death, it was often funny—like all John Green books—and

whimsical. For example, Hazel's favorite TV show is *America's Next Top Model.* Of course the book was also smart. Hazel and Augustus talk about philosophy, the meaning of life, and the meaning of suffering. References to literature pop up throughout the story, including the authors T. S. Eliot, J. D. Salinger, Emily Dickinson, and Shakespeare. The title is adapted from the Shakespeare play *Julius Caesar*, in which a character says, "The fault, dear Brutus, is not in our stars / But in ourselves."

In June, when Green tweeted the title of the book to his fans, it started to look as if he and his editor were right. Months before *TFIOS* (pronounced "TIFF-ee-ohs," as his fans had begun to call it) was even published, it was selling in numbers that none of his previous books had reached.

When it was published in January 2012, *TFIOS* debuted at No. 1 on the *New York Times* Best Seller list and remained at No. 1 for seven weeks. It has not dropped off the list in any of the weeks since then. Reviewers had very good things to say about the book. *Time* magazine said the novel was "near genius," and National Public Radio said the book "may be his best."

With the book getting him more attention than he'd ever had before, Green wanted to make sure to stay in touch with his most important fans: Nerdfighters. On January 10, 2012, the book's publication day, Green posted a vlogbrothers video. He answered Nerdfighters' questions while preparing to go on tour. One viewer asked what inspired him to write the book, and he explained that the story came from his experience volunteering at the children's hospital. He said he'd always wanted to write a story based on that experience. "It just took a while," Green explained. "A *long* while." Another viewer asked if he thought it was his best book. Green said he

Green signs fans' copies of *The Fault in Our Stars.*

couldn't judge that, but the reviews were better than for anything he'd published before.

One viewer asked Green if it was hard to write the book while also being a parent. "I don't think I could have written it *until* I was a parent," he said.

Green finished the video by thrusting a fist into the air and thanking everyone for reading the book. "I hope that you like it! DFTBA!" he said.

One thing Green had worried about was whether kids with cancer and their families would like the book. He worried they would think he didn't understand them well enough or didn't portray life with cancer accurately. But after publication, he began to hear from some kids living with cancer. Mostly they were supportive and appreciative of the book. They told him that he got the feeling of living with a terminal disease right. "It means a lot to me to read letters from kids who have cancer or other serious illnesses," Green said. "That's been the biggest surprise."

FROM THE LITTLE SCREEN TO THE BIG SCREEN

Soon movie producers began to call Green's agent to ask about buying the rights to make *TFIOS* into a movie. Green was very nervous about selling these rights. It was important to him that any movie stay faithful to the core of the book. He wanted to make sure that producers didn't add a happy ending or make the characters into heroes just because they are sick. He said, "People living with cancer are very much like people who are not living with cancer. They're every bit as funny and complex and diverse as anyone else." Green also felt that Hollywood movies often tended to look down on teens. "Hollywood doesn't treat teenagers as intelligent as they are," he noted.

Green was very involved in the production of the *TFIOS* film from the beginning. He was present as actors tried out to play his characters, and he enthusiastically approved when Shailene Woodley was cast as Hazel and Ansel Elgort was picked to play Augustus. He spent a great deal of time on the movie sets in both Pennsylvania and the Netherlands.

From left: John Green, Shailene Woodley, and Ansel Elgort stand arm in arm at a special event.

Characters Augustus and Hazel share a romantic moment in this scene from *The Fault in Our Stars.*

Green also put his typical energy into publicizing the movie. When the trailer was ready, he promoted it on his YouTube channel and on Twitter and Tumblr. By the time the movie came out in June 2014, the trailer had been viewed nearly 20 million times.

After the book had been out for a year, Green got one of the most exciting opportunities of his life. He and Hank put on a show at Carnegie Hall, a venue that has hosted thousands of legendary performers over the decades. The show, called "An Evening of Awesome," sold out the more than twenty-eight hundred tickets. John talked about his life and his work. Hank played a few of his songs, and the Mountain Goats—one of Green's favorite bands—played as well. Actors Ashley Clements and Daniel Vincent Gordh performed a dramatic reading from *TFIOS.* The author Neil Gaiman made a surprise appearance and participated in a Q&A with John and Hank.

Meanwhile, John and Hank continued to make videos, expanding their YouTube reach to new channels. One of those channels is Crash Course, in which John and Hank teach subjects that interest them. So far they've taught biology, world history, ecology, literature, chemistry, US history, and psychology.

Green kept busy caring for Henry and his new daughter, Alice, who was born in June 2013. But excitement over the *TFIOS* movie was growing. He did many interviews for magazines such as the *New Yorker*, *School Library Journal*, *Mental Floss*, and the *Wall Street Journal*. He even did an interview with his old mentor, Ilene Cooper, for *Booklist*.

By this time, Green's influence had grown to enormous heights. By the time the *TFIOS* movie came out, he had more than 2.5 million followers on Twitter, and the

Shailene Woodley and John Green promote *The Fault in Our Stars* with some help from a furry friend.

vlogbrothers YouTube channel had more than 2.1 million subscribers. In keeping with his usual dedication, Green posted a video from the world premiere of the movie. Hundreds of fans were lined up outside the theater.

Two days later, Hank posted a video in which he admitted to being overwhelmed by the attention he and his brother were getting lately, as well as how busy they'd been promoting the movie. "But there is one thing that I'm not worried about," Hank said. "I'm not worried that people won't like the movie . . . people are going to love it. And yeah, I cried. I cried a bunch of times, but not because it subtracted from me, but because it added to me. John, I'm proud of you."

One thing that journalists and fans kept asking Green was what he'd do next. *TFIOS* the book had been a major best seller for more than two years, with more than 9 million copies in print. The movie was the No. 1 box office hit in its first weekend. Did Green have another massive project up his sleeve?

"I do have other ideas," he said. "There [are] other things that I'm excited to write that are lighter . . . . This was an extremely difficult writing process, and I'd like to write something that's not so difficult next time. But I don't know. I want to take a little time off and catch my breath, figure out what I want to do next, and then do it."

Whatever his next project is, Green will no doubt pursue it with his usual hard work and humor. And millions of Nerdfighters will be waiting.

Important Dates

1977	John Green is born in Indianapolis, Indiana, on August 24.
1995	He graduates from Indian Springs boarding school in Indian Springs, Alabama, and begins attending Kenyon College in Gambier, Ohio.
2000	He graduates from Kenyon College and accepts a job in Chicago at *Booklist* after a brief stint as a chaplain at a children's hospital.
2005	His first novel, *Looking for Alaska*, is published.
2006	He marries Sarah Urist. *Looking for Alaska* wins the Printz Award. He publishes his second novel, *An Abundance of Katherines*.
2007	He starts communicating via vlog with his brother, Hank—a project that leads him to develop an enormous online following.
2008	He publishes his third novel, *Paper Towns*.

2009	He meets a teenage fan with thyroid cancer named Esther Grace Earl. The two become friends, and Esther helps inspire him to write a book about kids living with cancer.
2010	He publishes a fourth novel, *Will Grayson, Will Grayson*, with coauthor David Levithan. His son, Henry, is born.
2012	He publishes *The Fault in Our Stars*, a love story involving two teenagers with cancer. It quickly soars to No. 1 on the *New York Times* Best Seller list.
2013	His daughter, Alice, is born.
2014	The movie based on *The Fault in Our Stars* is released in June.

Source Notes

9   Jeffrey A. Trachtenberg, "Tweeting from a La-Z-Boy, an Unfinished Book Hits No. 1," *Wall Street Journal*, July 1, 2011, http://online.wsj.com/news/articles/SB10001424052702304450604576418161912396 81.

13 Margaret Talbot, "The Teen Whisperer," *New Yorker*, June 9, 2014, http://www.newyorker.com/reporting/2014/06/09/140609fa_fact_talbot?currentPage=all&mobify=0.

14 Ibid.

15 Jessica Grose, "The Green Movement," *Mental Floss*, January 15, 2014, http://mentalfloss.com/article/54509/green-movement.

16 John Green, "Nick (from All Things Considered)," *John Green*, May 26, 2003, http://johngreenbooks.com/nick-from-all-things -considered/.

16 Marc McEvoy, "Interview: John Green," *Sydney Morning Herald*, January 21, 2012, http://www.smh.com.au/entertainment/books /interview-john-green-20120119-1q71w.html.

17 Grose, "The Green Movement."

18 "Perspective," YouTube video, 3:29, posted by "vlogbrothers," October 29, 2013, https://www.youtube.com /watch?v=5ooCeoh66o8.

19 Ibid.

22 "Brotherhood 2.0: January 1st," YouTube video, 2:02, posted by "vlogbrothers," accessed July 7, 2014, https://www.youtube.com /watch?v=vtyXbTHKhI0.

24–25 "Brotherhood 2.0: February 17, 2007," YouTube video, 3:13, posted by "vlogbrothers," February 15, 2007, https://www.youtube.com/watch?v=tuvCb5eBbjE.

27 "December 3rd: 10,000 Subscribers! and Secret Project," YouTube video, 3:36, posted by "vlogbrothers," December 3, 2007, https://www.youtube.com/watch?v=jcwr4-dImCQ.

29–30 Ilene Cooper, "A Conversation with John Green & Ilene Cooper," *Booklist*, January 1, 2012, http://www.booklistonline.com/ProductInfo.aspx?pid=5217539&AspxAutoDetectCookieSupport=1.

30–31 Jade Chang, "Interview with John Green," *Goodreads*, December 2012, accessed June 3, 2014, http://www.goodreads.com/interviews/show/828.John_Green.

32 McEvoy, "Interview: John Green."

34 Lev Grossman, "The Topic of Cancer: A Young-Adult Novel That Triumphs with Humor and Pathos," *Time*, February 6, 2012. http://content.time.com/time/magazine/article/0,9171,2105454,00.html

34 Rachel Syme, "'The Fault in Our Stars': Love in a Time of Cancer," *NPR*, January 17, 2012, http://www.npr.org/2012/01/17/145343351/the-fault-in-our-stars-love-in-a-time-of-cancer.

35 "The Fault in Our Stars," YouTube video, 3:27, posted by "vlogbrothers," January 10, 2012, https://www.youtube.com/watch?v=g_FzrUXOZEc.

35 Chang, "Interview with John Green."

36 McEvoy, "Interview: John Green."

36 Andy Lewis, "'Fault in Our Stars' Author John Green: Why He's 'Freaking Out' about Hollywood Success," *Hollywood Reporter*, May 1, 2014, http://www.hollywoodreporter.com/news/fault -stars-author-john-green-699388.

39 "Thoughts from the TFiOS Premiere!" YouTube video, 3:58, posted by "vlogbrothers," June 6, 2014, https://www.youtube .com/watch?v=KncQ2AnsFEQ.

39 Cooper. "A Conversation."

Selected Bibliography

Alter, Alexandra. "John Green and His Nerdfighters Are Upending the Summer Blockbuster Model." *Wall Street Journal*, May 14, 2014. http://online.wsj.com/news/articles/SB10001424052702304431104579552173066169420?mg=reno64-wsj&turl=http%3A%2F%2Fonline.wsj.com%2Farticle%2FSB10001424052702304431104579552173066169420.html.

"Brotherhood 2.0, February 17, 2007." YouTube video. 3:13. Posted by "vlogbrothers," February 15, 2007. http://www.youtube.com/watch?v=tuvCb5eBbjE.

Cooper, Ilene. "A Conversation with John Green & Ilene Cooper." *Booklist*, January 1, 2012. http://www.booklistonline.com/ProductInfo.aspx?pid=5217539&AspxAutoDetectCookieSupport=1.

Grose, Jessica. "The Green Movement." *Mental Floss*, January 15, 2014. http://mentalfloss.com/article/54509/green-movement.

"Hospital Chaplain: The Miracle of Swindon Town #33." YouTube video. 11:57. Posted by "hankgames," November 2, 2011. https://www.youtube.com/watch?v=1udWGw7KsIc.

McEvoy, Marc. "Interview: John Green." *Sydney Morning Herald*, January 21, 2012. http://www.smh.com.au/entertainment/books/interview-john-green-20120119-1q71w.html.

"My Life as a Child: The Miracle of Swindon Town #48." YouTube video. 12:47. Posted by "hankgames," November 25, 2011. https://www.youtube.com/watch?v=_4LJ6BxlVnI.

Talbot, Margaret. "The Teen Whisperer." *New Yorker*, June 9, 2014. http://www.newyorker.com/reporting/2014/06/09/140609fa_fact_talbot?currentPage=all&mobify=0.

"Thoughts from the TFiOS Premiere!" YouTube video. 3:58. Posted by "vlogbrothers," June 6, 2014. http://www.youtube.com /watch?v=KncQ2AnsFEQ.

Trachtenberg, Jeffrey A. "Tweeting from a La-Z-Boy, an Unfinished Book Hits No. 1." *Wall Street Journal*, July 1, 2011. http://online.wsj.com /s/news/articles/SB10001424052702304450604576418161912396814.

Further Reading

Books

Green, John. *The Fault in Our Stars*. New York: Dutton, 2012. Read the heart-wrenching yet uplifting story of Hazel Grace Lancaster and Augustus Waters, two teens with cancer who fall deeply in love.

——. *Looking for Alaska*. New York, Dutton, 2005. Check out John Green's first novel, a semiautobiographical story about a bullied teen who finds his place at a boarding school but faces tragedy along the way.

Schwartz, Heather E. *Shailene Woodley: Divergent's Daring Star*. Minneapolis: Lerner Publications, 2015. Read this fun biography of Shailene Woodley, star of *The Fault in Our Stars* as well as *Divergent*, another popular YA novel turned movie.

Websites

John Green
http://johngreenbooks.com
Fans of the author will want to make sure to pay his website a visit.

Vlogbrothers
https://www.youtube.com/user/vlogbrothers
Learn more about John Green and see great videos at the website he runs with his brother.

Index

An Abundance of Katherines, 21

Booklist, 16–20, 38
Brotherhood 2.0, 22–28
bullying, 12–13, 20

chaplaincy, 15–16
Cooper, Ilene, 17, 19, 38
Crash Course, 38

depression, 13, 17–19
DFTBA ("Don't forget to be awesome"), 26–27, 35
divinity school, 15–16

Earl, Esther Grace, 29–32
Elgort, Ansel, 36–37
"An Evening of Awesome," 37

Fault in Our Stars, The (book), 7–10, 32–35, 39
Fault in Our Stars, The (film), 35–39

Green, Alice, 38
Green, Hank, 9, 11, 22–28, 31, 37–39
Green, Henry, 31, 38
Green, Sarah Urist. *See* Urist, Sarah

Harvey, 18–19

Indianapolis, IN, 10, 29
Indian Springs, 13, 17, 20, 22
interviews, 38

Kenyon College, 14–15
Kluge, P. F., 14–15

LeakyCon, 28–29
Looking for Alaska, 19–20

Nerdfighters, 9–10, 24–27, 34, 39
New York Times Best Seller list, 33–34

Orlando, FL, 10–11, 18
Ott, Bill, 17–18

Paper Towns, 28
Printz Award, 19, 21
Project for Awesome, 27–28

Strauss-Gabel, Julie, 32

therapy, 18–19
tweets, 7–8, 33
Twitter, 7–9, 37, 38

Urist, Sarah, 20–21, 29, 31

VidCon, 31
vlogbrothers, 26, 28, 31, 34, 39

Will Grayson, Will Grayson, 28–29
Woodley, Shailene, 36–37, 38

YouTube, 8–9, 22–23, 27, 37–39